VOLUME 11

SING WITH THE CHOIR

CD INCLUDED

CHRISTMAS TIME IS HERE

Visit Hal Leonard Online at
www.halleonard.com

T0078957

ISBN: 978-1-4234-5815-9

DISTRIBUTED BY

HAL•LEONARD®
CORPORATION
7777 W. BLUEMOUND RD. P.O. BOX 13819 MILWAUKEE, WI 53213

Visit Hal Leonard Online at
www.halleonard.com

CONTENTS

Blue Christmas

Arranged by
MAC HUFF

Words and Music by BILLY HAYES
and JAY JOHNSON

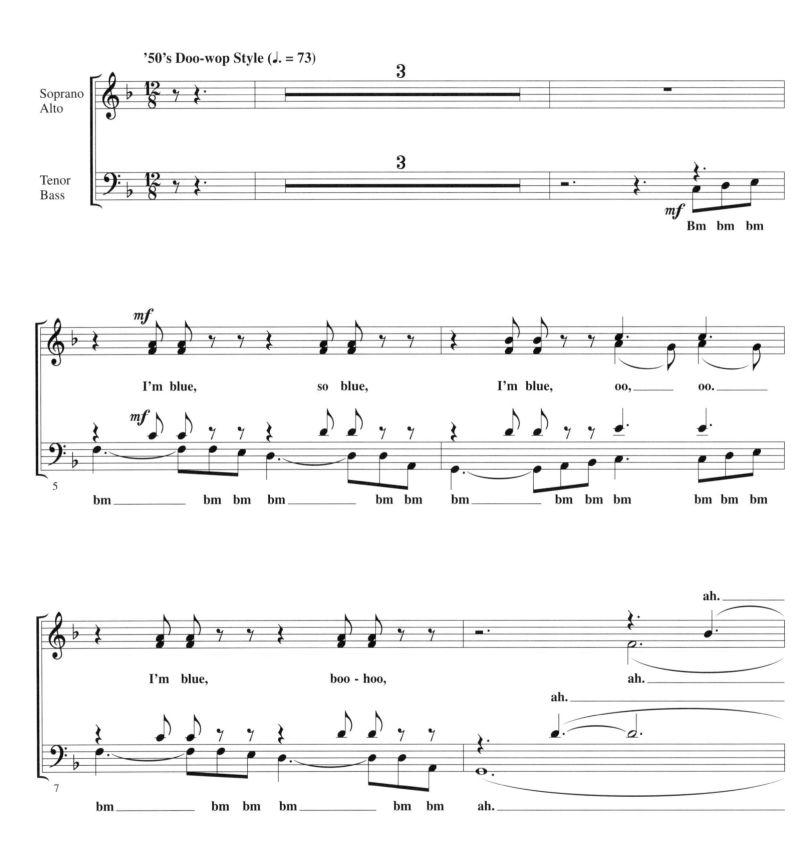

ra - tions of red____ on a green Christ - mas tree_____

won't mean a thing_____ if you're not here with me.

And_____ when_____ the blue

Doo wop, doo wop,

Bm bm bm bm_____ bm bm bm_____ bm bm

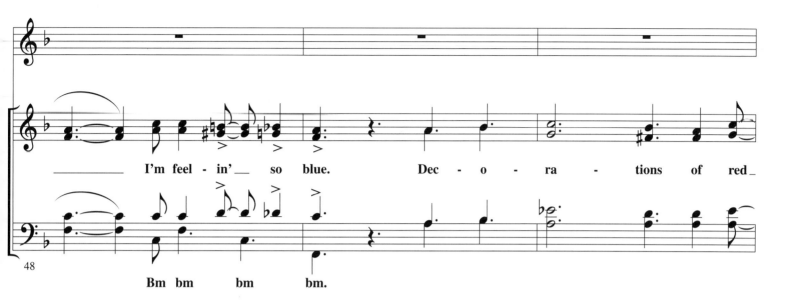

I'm feel - in'___ so blue. Dec - o - ra - tions of red___

Bm bm bm bm.

___ on a green Christ - mas tree___

won't mean a thing___ if you're not here with me.

cresc.

cresc.

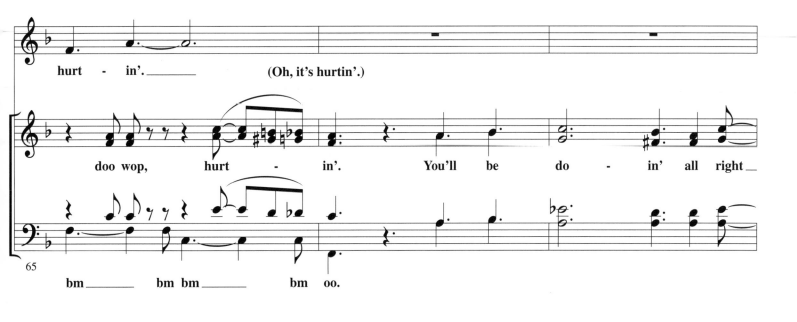

hurt - in'. _____ (Oh, it's hurtin'.)

doo wop, hurt - in'. You'll be do - in' all right __

bm _____ bm bm _____ bm oo.

65

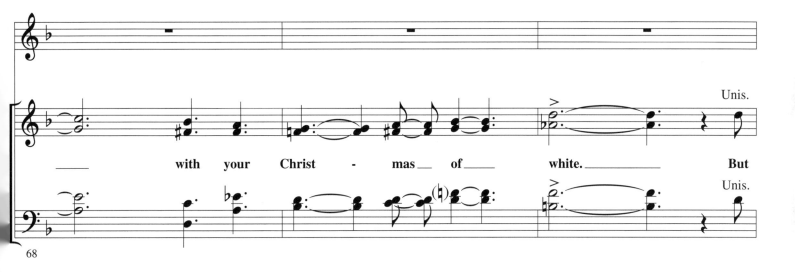

_____ with your Christ - mas __ of _____ white. _____ But

with your Christ - mas __ of _____ white. _____ But

Unis.

Unis.

68

rit.

But I'll _____ have a blue, blue

rit. e dim.

I'll _____ have a blue, blue Christ - mas. _____

rit. e dim.

71

Christmas Time Is Here

**Arranged by
STEVE ZEGREE**

**Words by LEE MENDELSON
Music by VINCE GUARALDI**

16

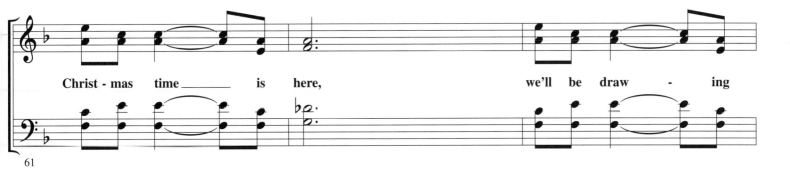

Christ - mas time _____ is here, we'll be draw - ing

Oh, that we _____ could al - ways see _____ such

near; Oh, that we could al - ways see such

Oh, that we _____ could

div. div. rit.

spir - it through the year. Oh, that we could

rit.

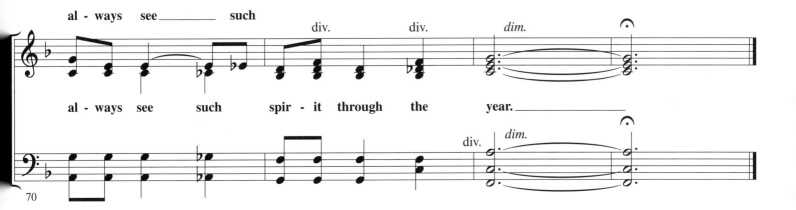

al - ways see _____ such div. div. dim.

al - ways see such spir - it through the year. _____

div. dim.

Feliz Navidad

Arranged by
MAC HUFF

Music and Lyrics by
JOSE FELICIANO

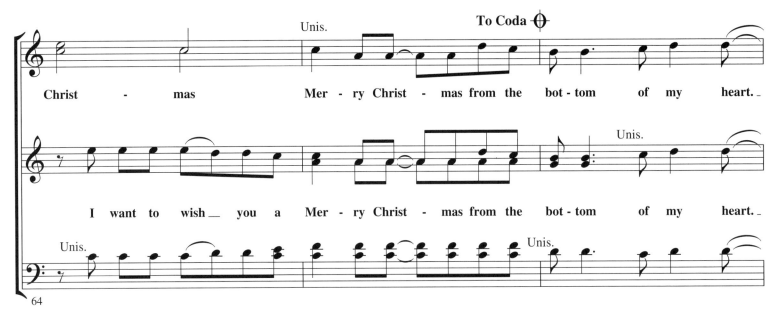

Christ - mas   Mer - ry Christ - mas from the bot - tom of my heart.

I want to wish __ you a Mer - ry Christ - mas from the bot - tom of my heart.

64

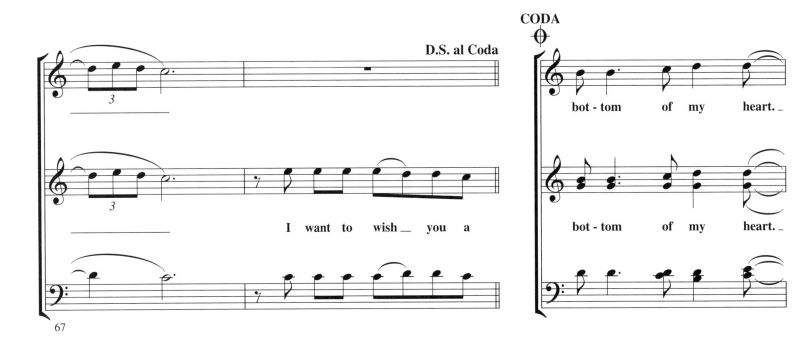

D.S. al Coda

CODA

I want to wish __ you a

bot - tom of my heart.

bot - tom of my heart.

67

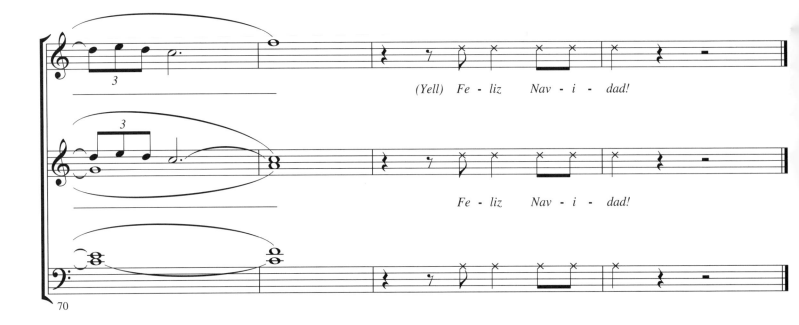

(Yell) Fe - liz Nav - i - dad!

Fe - liz Nav - i - dad!

70

I'll Be Home for Christmas

Arranged by
ED LOJESKI

Words and Music by **KIM GANNON**
and **WALTER KENT**

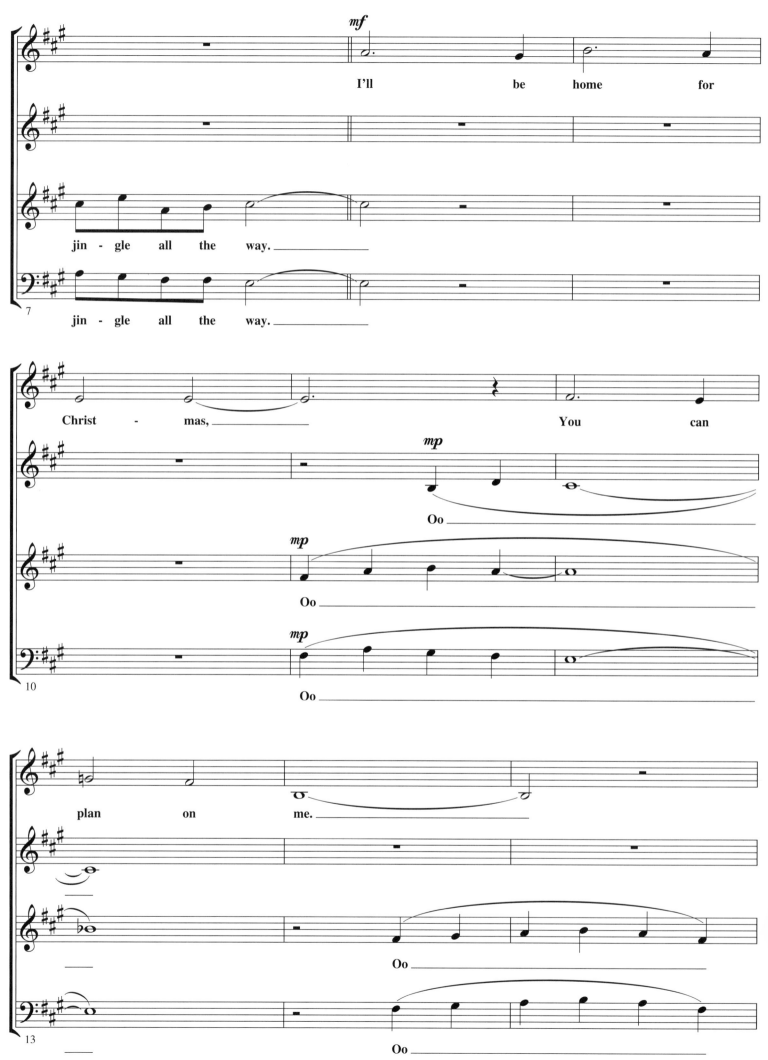

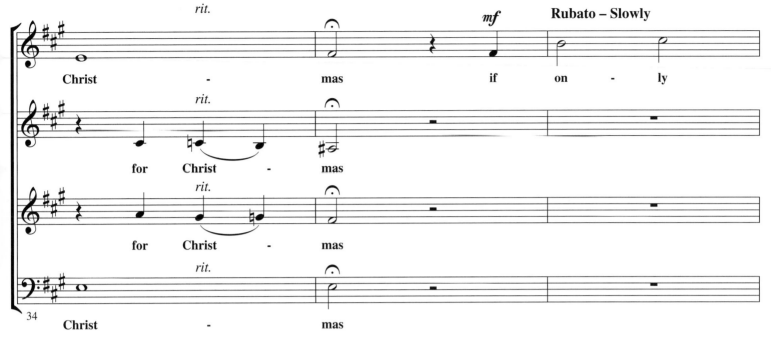

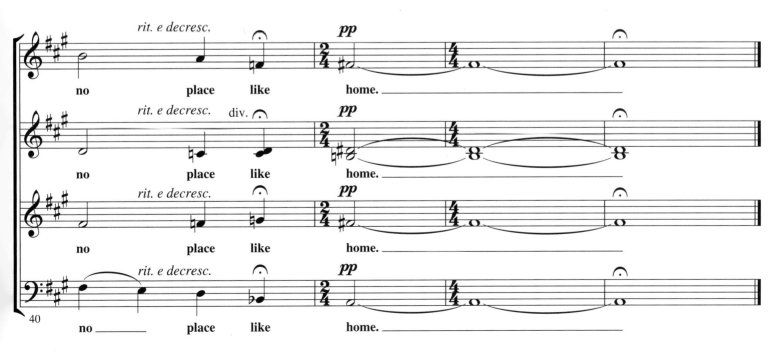

Happy Xmas
(War Is Over)

Arranged by
MARK BRYMER

Words and Music by **JOHN LENNON**
and **YOKO ONO**

fear.　　　　　　And so this is Christ-mas___

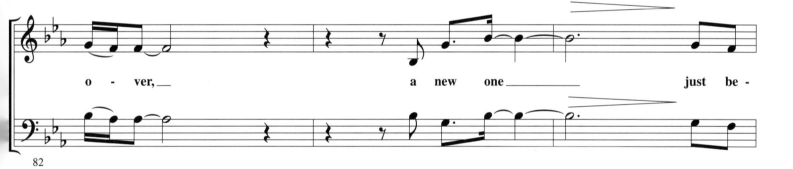

and what have__ we__ done?　　　An - oth - er year

o - ver,___　　　　a new one_____　　just be -

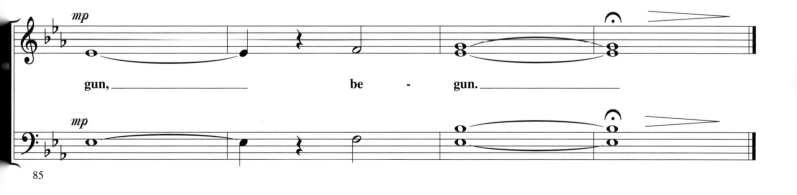

gun,_____　　be - gun._____

Let It Snow! Let It Snow! Let It Snow!

**Arranged by
KIRBY SHAW**

Words by SAMMY CAHN
Music by JULE STYNE

*Begin glissando on last half of beat 2

38

some corn for pop-pin', and the lights____ are turned way down low,____

63

End Duet **D.S. al Coda**

_____ let it snow,____ let it snow,__ let it snow!

All - Unis. *mf*

When we

66

CODA

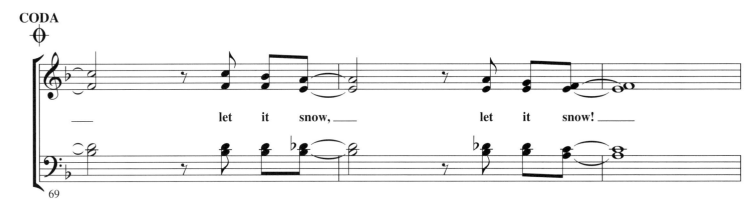

__ let it snow,____ let it snow!_____

69

Unis.

Let it snow!__ Let it snow!__ Let it snow!__ Let it snow!__

Unis.

72

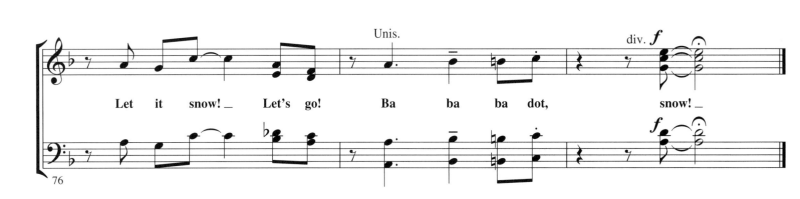

Unis.

div. *f*

Let it snow!__ Let's go! Ba ba ba dot, snow!__

f

76

We Need a Little Christmas

Arranged by
MAC HUFF

Music and Lyric by
JERRY HERMAN

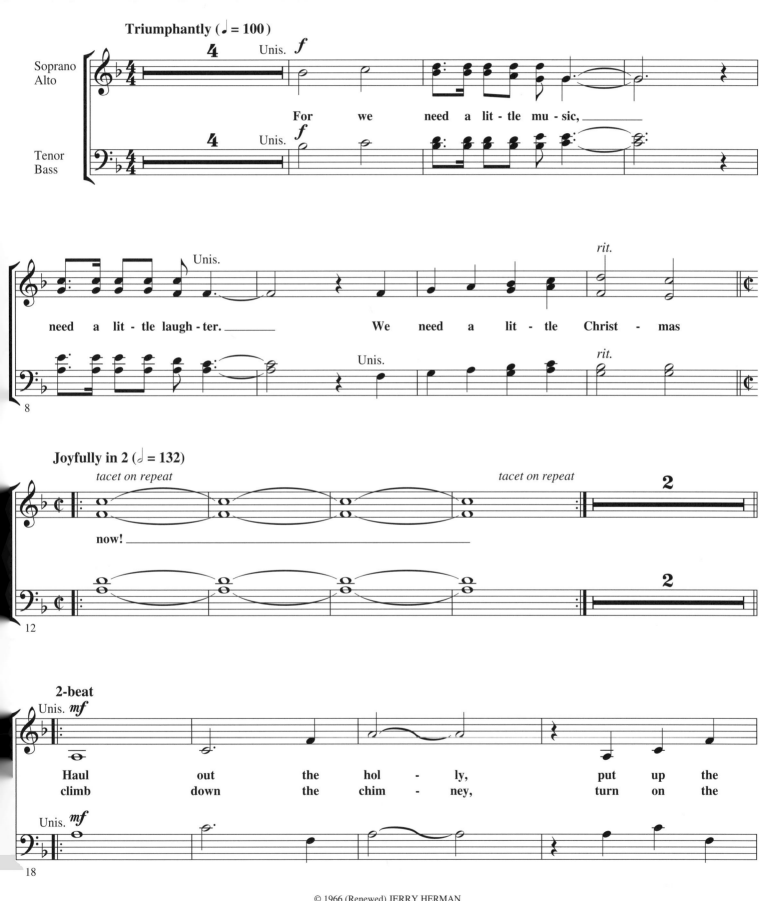

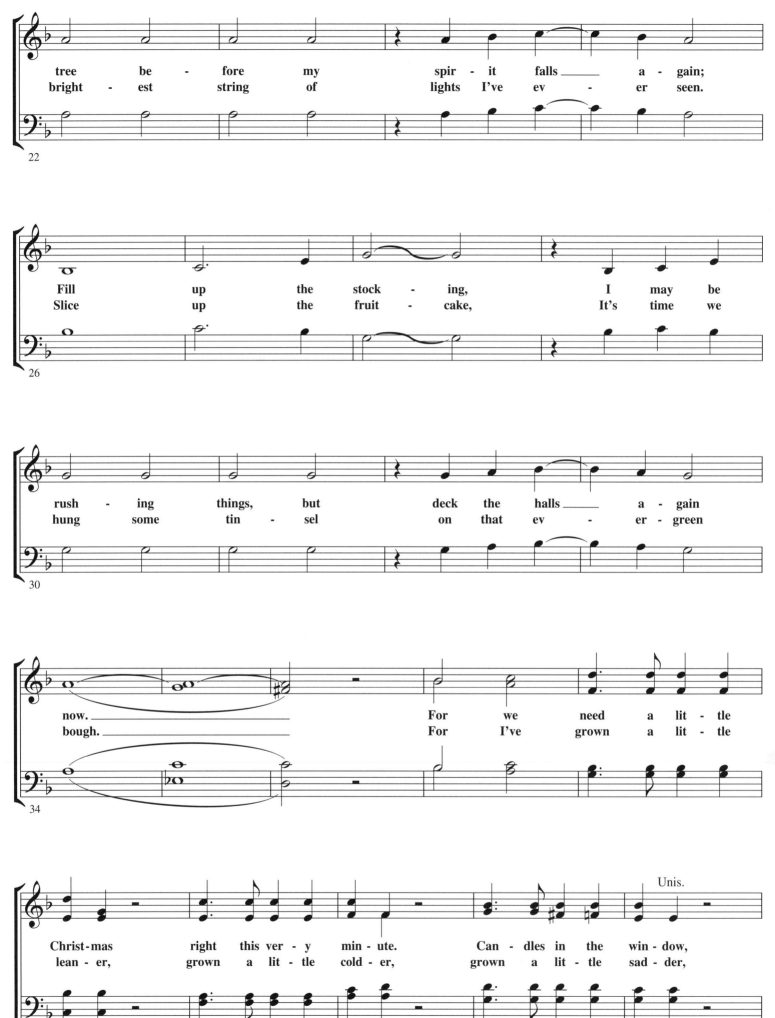

car - ols at the spin - et. Yes, we need a lit - tle Christ - mas
grown a lit - tle old - er. And I need a lit - tle an - gel

right this ver - y min - ute. It has - n't snowed a sin - gle flur - ry, But
sit - ting on my shoul - der.

San - ta, dear, we're in a hur - ry. So Need a lit - tle

Christ - mas, need a lit - tle Christ -

mas now! _____

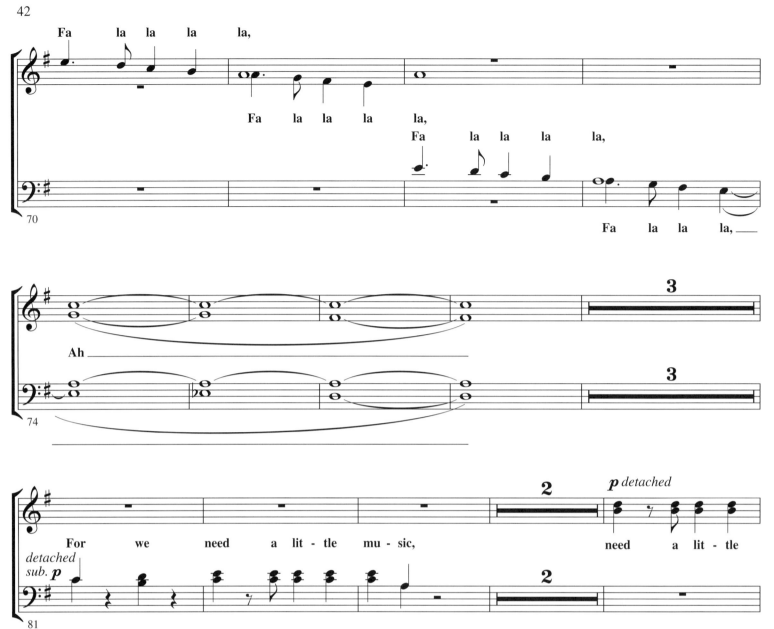

42

Fa la la la la,
Fa la la la la,
Fa la la la la,
Fa la la la, ___

70

Ah ___

74

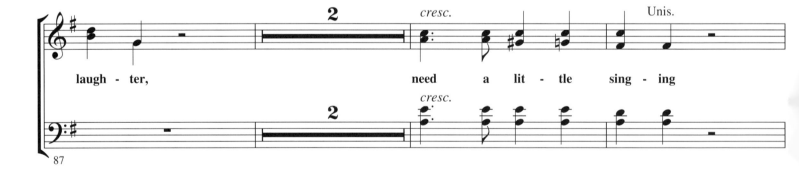

detached
sub. *p*
For we need a lit - tle mu - sic, *p detached* need a lit - tle

81

laugh - ter, *cresc.* need a lit - tle sing - ing *Unis.*

87

ring - ing through the raft - er. And we need a lit - tle snap - py
Unis. *f*

92

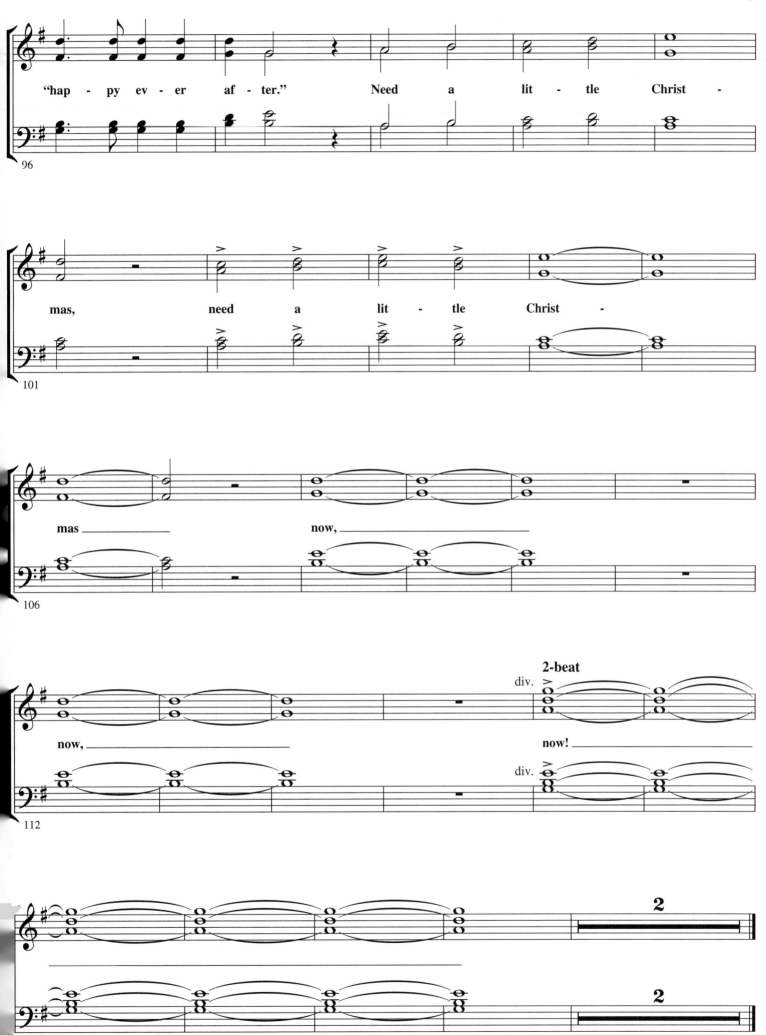

"hap - py ev - er af - ter." Need a lit - tle Christ -

mas, need a lit - tle Christ -

mas _____ now, _____

now, _____ now!

Wonderful Christmastime

Arranged by
ALAN BILLINGSLEY

Words and Music by
PAUL McCARTNEY

46